THE
BATTLE
OF
TRENTON

By

SAMUEL STELLE SMITH

PHILIP FRENEAU PRESS

MONMOUTH BEACH, N. J.

1965

WASHINGTON CROSSING THE DELAWARE This famous painting by Emanuel Leutze (1816-1868) was completed in 1851. It was quickly acclaimed and exhibited in the United States Capitol. It is a large painting, 21 x 12 feet, and is now on exhibit in the Memorial Building, Washington Crossing State Park, Pennsylvania. It is one of two known paintings of the same title by Leutze. The second one, after having been slightly damaged by fire and repaired by the artist, was sold to the German government in 1863, and later hung in Bremen Kunsthalle. It was destroyed by a British bombing raid on September 15, 1942. Emanuel Leutze was born in Germany and came to America with his parents when he was nine. He grew up in Philadelphia and went to Europe to study art in 1841, age 25. This painting was executed in Dusseldorf, Germany, just before returning to the United States in 1851. This painting is on loan from the Metropolitan Museum of Art, New York.

Copyright 1965 S. S. Smith L. C. no. 65-28860

FOREWORD

The Battle of Trenton was not the turn of the tide of the American Revolutionary War, as generations of historians have tried to prove. Seven years of exhausting war had to come before the peace-treaty of Paris stopped bloodshed in the newly born United States. Battles of Long Island, Brandywine, Saratoga, Monmouth, Charleston, Guilford Court-House, and Yorktown marked the story of this war.

The grand strategy of war was not changed by the Battle of Trenton, but it was this little town on the east bank of the Delaware, where the Continental Army and militia gained their first victory over Hessian veterans of the allied army, who had demoralized the American soldiers during all engagements before. The ideas of liberty and independence rose again after that glorious Christmas Day 1776.

Due to this fact, a web of romantic and patriotic feeling on the American side and of self-accusations and corrections on the Hessian side, was cast over the story of this battle. Thus, historiography has failed to show us a clear picture of the events surrounding Trenton.

Basing his study on both German and American sources, Samuel Stelle Smith found a convincing way of describing the battle and of analyzing the scenery by historical evidence. Subjective historical emotion is not to be found in this book that puts the Battle of Trenton at its proper place in history.

Munich, Germany, October 1965

Dr. Ernst Kipping

AUTHOR'S PREFACE

This book is the second of a series on the battles of the Revolutionary War in the middle states. The Battle of Monmouth, published in 1964, was well accepted and encouraged the writer to continue. The battles of Trenton and Princeton seemed to be the most logical next step.

Traditionally, these two battles have been handled as one, because they were fought only one week apart in the same general area. As the material developed, this time and place factor seemed to be the only element these two battles had in common. Then, about halfway through the research, it was decided to separate the two conflicts into two books, one to be published in 1965 and the other in 1966.

At Trenton, on December 26, 1776, there was not one British soldier in the battle, but at Princeton on January 3, 1777, the British did all of the fighting for their side. At Trenton, the Rall brigade of Hessians handled the entire affair for the British, but at Princeton, the Rall brigade was no more.

On the American side there was a similar separation of effort. At Trenton, the divisions of Generals Greene and Sullivan did all of the fighting and Generals Cadwalader and Ewing failed to arrive on the battlefield. But at Princeton, these absentee generals were in the hardest fighting.

Thus, by this set of circumstances, the author was led down the path to a series on the Revolution, which is now enlarged to a planned five volumes to include The Battle of Princeton, Bloody New Jersey the Revolutionary War Pawn and The Philadelphia Campaign.

WASHINGTON AT TRENTON AND PRINCETON *This oil portrait is by Charles Willson Peale of Philadelphia (1741-1827). Peale was a lieutenant with Gen. Cadwalader's Philadelphia militia and participated with Cadwalader at Trenton and at Princeton, a week later. Peale knew Washington well, both as a civilian and as an officer. For this remarkable portrait, Washington posed for Peale between January 20 and February 1, 1779. In the foreground, lower left, are shown Hessian flags and cannon captured at Trenton. In the right foreground is a red British ensign captured at Princeton. (There were no British flags or troops captured at Trenton). The flag behind the horse's head is Gen. Washington's headquarters flag, with a blue background and 13 white stars. In the background are shown blue-coated American soldiers guarding red-coated British soldiers captured at Princeton; and on the horizon can be seen steepled Nassau Hall at Princeton. The captured flags and cannon were painted by Peale from personal observation and sketches. Peale made several copies of this portrait of Washington. The original is owned by the Pennsylvania Academy of Fine Arts, Philadelphia. Replicas are owned by Colonial Williamsburg and Princeton University.*

4

CHAPTER ONE

WASHINGTON RETREATS

Ten Against Three

On December first, 1776, at 1:30 p.m., General George Washington wrote to the Continental Congress, which was in session in Philadelphia, that "The Enemy are fast advancing, some of 'em are now in sight." The general was writing from Brunswick, now New Brunswick, New Jersey. Soon the British brought up cannon to the heights across the Raritan River and began firing into the town.

General Washington returned the fire, but even while the cannonade continued he wrote a second letter to Congress. "It being impossible to oppose them with our present force with the least prospect of success, we shall retreat to the West side of [the] Delaware." Washington himself remained in Brunswick until 7:30 p.m. or later, but by that hour some of his force was eight miles south of Brunswick and about half way to Princeton.

General Washington's force, as it left Brunswick, was 3000 men; his "4000 men" of the day before having been reduced by one quarter through expiring enlistments effective November 30. The British force before which Gen. Washington was retreating numbered approximately 10,000 men, a ratio of 10 to 3. (See Appendix A)

Before riding out of Brunswick, General Washington sent an urgent message to Major General Charles Lee, second in command of the American army. Gen. Lee was at Peekskill, New York with a force of "about 2000 men." To Lee, Washington wrote, "I must entreat you to hasten your march, as much as possible, or your arrival may be too late to answer any valuable purpose. Your route nor the place to join me I cannot particularize. In these instances we must be governed by Circumstances."

Gen. Washington arrived at Princeton between eight and nine o'clock in the morning on December 2, about the same time his troops entered the town. At Princeton, General Washington decided to post a rear guard of approximately half of his small army to watch the enemy and give notice of their approach. A second purpose was to protect Gen. Lee's flank should he try to join Gen. Washington on the New Jersey side of the Delaware. The force left behind at Princeton consisted of two brigades totalling "1200 men," under Brigadier General Lord Stirling (William Alexander) and Brigadier General Adam Stephen.

Washington and the balance of his force must have spent little time in Princeton on the 2nd, for the general and some of his army arrived at Trenton, twelve miles south, before noon. Immediately, headquarters were established and preparations were made to move supplies and equipment across the Delaware. Washington had anticipated the need of boats for this purpose, and while still at Brunswick, he had written to Colonel Richard Humpton in Pennsylvania to assemble at Trenton boats necessary to transport troops and baggage across the river, and to secure all other boats on the west side of the Delaware.

At about the same time Gen. Washington entered Trenton from the north, another body of troops entered the town from the south. This small detachment of 26 dragoons was the 1st troop of Philadelphia city cavalry, which had left Philadelphia December 1. Their number was not large but they brought the heartening news that 1500 additional Philadelphia militia were on the march to join the fight.

Samuel Morris was the captain of the Philadelphia cavalry troop and Benjamin Randolph, the famous Philadelphia cabinet-maker, was one of the privates. Within a short time, Pvt. Benjamin Randolph was at general headquarters asking to see the commander-in-chief. Soon Pvt. Randolph and Gen. Washington were together and their first subject of conversation probably was not military affairs, but Philadelphia and the health of Mrs. Washington.

The general's wife had not seen her husband since early summer, when he had been in Philadelphia attending Congress for several days. He had left her at Randolph's Chestnut Street home in Philadelphia when he "went away June 5th." Mrs. Washington departed for Virginia a few days later, but soon returned north to spend a month or two with her husband in New York.

Instead, she was forced to remain most of the summer and fall at the Randolphs' while the British army landed on Staten Island, crossed to Long Island and defeated Washington there, then moved over the East River and took New York. Washington had many things indeed to talk over with Randolph on the morning of the 2nd.

During the afternoon of the 2nd, Gen. Washington wrote two short letters, one of which was his almost daily report to Congress. To them he wrote, "When the Enemy first landed on this side of the North [Hudson] River, I apprehended that they meant to make a push this way." Washington's apprehension had now become a reality. After the fall of New York, Washington had to withdraw to Harlem Heights, then to White Plains, and to Peekskill in Westchester County, New York. On November 13, he crossed over the North River with his troops at Peekskill and started his painful retreat to Hackensack, to Newark, to Elizabethtown, arriving at Brunswick on November 29.

British Change Plans

The British force in New Jersey, which was pursuing Gen. Washington was not originally a force of 10,000 men. The units which departed New York on November 19, and landed at Alpine, New Jersey, early the next morning, totaled "about 4000 men," approximately the same strength as Gen. Washington's New Jersey force on that date. But many more troops were to come, not to fight but to enjoy "good winter quarters in New Jersey." Food and forage were also considerations but most important was the fact that the British would be in position in the spring for General Sir William Howe to "advance the army across the Delaware and march to Philadelphia."

On November 25, the 2nd and 4th British brigades crossed over the North River, and on the 28th Rall's brigade of

Hessians crossed over. In less than a week, British forces in New Jersey had more than doubled.

With such a strong force in New Jersey, the British could have pushed on to Trenton and caused great damage to Washington's withdrawal across the Delaware. But Gen. Howe had given orders "not to advance beyond Brunswick," in their search for suitable winter quarters.

Then about December 3, plans were changed, and British forces in New Jersey were ordered to advance to the Delaware, possibly to Philadelphia. The reason for this sudden change in tactics appears to have been that "General Howe became possessed of a letter . . . written by General Washington to the Board of War, in which he had given an exact account when the time of service of all of our battalions would expire, and his apprehensions that the men would not reinlist without first going home to see their families and friends."

On December 4, the heavy rain that fell over a large area seemed to have a delaying effect on all New Jersey operations. General Lee complained of it as far north as Haverstraw, New York, where he seemed to hesitate after crossing over the North River on December 2.

On the 5th, the weather having cleared, Gen. Washington completed the task of moving his baggage and stores across the Delaware, and Lieutenant Colonel Stephen Kemble, deputy adjutant general of the British army in North America, entered in his journal at New York, "General Howe went to Jersey."

Gen. Howe arrived in Brunswick on the 6th, and the next morning the whole of Major General Earl Charles Cornwallis' division, with the exception of the two battalions of Guards, moved south to take "the advantage that might be gained by pushing on to the Delaware and the possibility of getting to Philadelphia." The Guards were left at Brunswick to protect supplies. All other troops were on the march out of Brunswick by dark on the 7th.

As the British were getting well under way in their march south on the 7th, Gen. Washington, who was somewhat puzzled at the week's delay of British forces at Brunswick, started out from Trenton with a force of about 500 men to reinforce his two brigades at Princeton. Soon, however, his plan was halted by the receipt of a message that the enemy was advancing by different roads, a possible attempt to get in the rear of the troops at Princeton. Washington called for an immediate retreat of all forces to Trenton, then a withdrawal across the Delaware.

At Princeton, which the British entered with little resistance, Gen. Howe divided his force into two corps. "General Howe marched to Trenton with Reserves, 4th Brigade, Light Infantry 2 Battalions, and three Battalions Hessian Grenadiers." Major General James Grant was the field officer in command of the troops which advanced on Trenton. The balance of the British forces in that theater, under Maj. Gen. Cornwallis, stopped at Maidenhead, now Lawrenceville, about half way between Princeton and Trenton.

Before withdrawing over the Delaware with the last of his troops, Gen. Washington sent a small detachment south to take up all bridges within a distance of three or four miles below Trenton. Then he gave up the town. In Gen. Howe's words, the British force "reached the Delaware soon after the enemy's rear guard had crossed."

CHAPTER TWO

RIVER BARRIER

Cornwallis Attempts Crossing

The day after General Howe's arrival in Trenton, plans were being made for British forces to push across the Delaware and take Philadelphia, the capital of The United States.

Generals Howe and Grant occupied Trenton where there were two ferries, one below the town, named Trenton Ferry, and a smaller one just above the town. Four miles above Trenton, two ferries also were in operation. In New Jersey, operating from near the foot of Upper Ferry Road, it was Howell's Ferry, and in Pennsylvania it was Yardley's Ferry, now Yardley.

Gen. Cornwallis was at Maidenhead, almost directly east of another principal ferry crossing, eight miles above Trenton. Here likewise there were two ferries, possibly three. (See Appendix B) From the New Jersey side it was Johnson's or John's Ferry, and from the Pennsylvania side it was Mc Konkey's Ferry, now Washington Crossing. It seemed apparent that an attempt to cross the Delaware would be made at one or more of these places.

The "next morning [December 9] at one o'clock" a.m., Gen. Cornwallis made almost an about-face and marched his division in darkness from Maidenhead to Coryell's Ferry, now Lambertville, New Jersey, 15 miles above Trenton. This was to be the main British effort to cross the Delaware.

Gen. Washington had anticipated a possible move in the direction of Coryell's. He wrote to Congress earlier, "if they cross at Corrill's Ferry or thereabouts, they are as near to Philadelphia as we are here." To meet this threat, Wash-

WILLIAM TRENT HOUSE *This lovely Queen Anne style brick mansion was built for William Trent in 1719. It was William Trent, Chief Justice of New Jersey in 1723, for whom the city of Trenton was named. The mansion was occupied by the Trents until his death in 1724. At the time of the Battle of Trenton, the property was occupied by Dr. William Bryant, and from December 17, 1776 to December 26, 1776, it was the headquarters of a detachment of one officer and 30 Hessian soldiers. The house, located on South Warren Street, Trenton, is presently a museum with 17th and 18th century furnishings. It is operated by The Trent House Association.*

ington had sent to Coryell's the newly arrived German regiment of about 400 men from Pennsylvania and Maryland under Colonel Nicholas Haussegger. Washington was aware that Col. Haussegger could not hold off a large force, but expected that he could delay a crossing attempt until Washington could "bring our Cannon up to play upon them."

On the morning that Gen. Cornwallis was making his forced march to Coryell's, but without knowledge of Cornwallis' movements, Washington ordered the main part of his army deployed along the Delaware between Coryell's and Yardley's Ferries. Instructions to his generals were: "Quarter Brigades in Houses or Hutts as compactly as possibly . . . Each Brigadier is to take care of his own Front, and keep strong Guards at all convenient passing places; the intermediate spaces between the Brigades, are to be attended by the Brigadiers next adjoining."

Brigadier General Mathieu Alexis Roche de Fermoy, a recent volunteer from France, was to cover the area around Coryell's Ferry. Col. Haussegger would be allowed to keep his post at the ferry proper but, upon Gen. Roche de Fermoy's arrival at the post, Haussegger's regiment would be annexed to the Fermoy brigade.

Gen. Stirling was to headquarter two miles below Coryell's and watch Beaumont's in Pennsylvania and nearby Cox's Ferry in New Jersey. Gen. Stephen, next below, would cover McKonkey's Ferry and Johnson's Ferry. Brigadier General Hugh Mercer was to be below Gen. Stephen.

Gen. Cornwallis arrived with his force at Coryell's Ferry at daybreak the 9th, and found Col. Haussegger waiting for him. Although Gen. Cornwallis failed in his attempt to cross the Delaware that morning, it was not Col. Haussegger who prevented his crossing, but the river itself. Cornwallis had not brought his own boats and Washington had seen to it that there were none there for him. Cornwallis' unpreparedness was undoubtedly due to the change in plans to cross immediately, rather than in the spring. Cornwallis spent the day searching for boats, then on the 10th returned south and went into bivouac at Pennington, north of Trenton.

While the Cornwallis crossing attempt was in motion, Gen. Washington was at "Berkleys Summer seat," his headquarters 15 miles down river from Coryell's. This was the summer home of Mr. Thomas Barclay of Philadelphia, located across from Trenton, about half a mile from the Delaware at what is now Morrisville, Pennsylvania.

At 9 a.m. on the morning of the 10th, about the time Cornwallis started his return south, Washington received word that the enemy was repairing the bridges below Trenton. Washington wrote to Congress that the move "seems to indicate an intention of their passing lower down."

Washington also wrote to the Pennsylvania Council of Safety ordering Commodore Thomas Seymour of the Pennsylvania state navy to send one of his galleys up river as far as Dunk's (Duncan Williams) Ferry, just below Neshaminy Creek, so that it might give the earliest information on enemy movements in that area. Col. Humpton who carried the message to the Council of Safety was ordered to proceed to Cooper's Creek, opposite Philadelphia, and Rancocas Creek, a little farther north, and bring down to Philadelphia all craft he could find there.

Washington now seemed certain that the British were going to push down the New Jersey side of the Delaware and cross over to Philadelphia at or near Camden. The general closed his letter to the Council of Safety with the following: "Having sent down Major General [Israel] Putnam to throw up necessary Works for the Defense of your City, I hope you will co-operate with him."

In a third letter that morning, Washington wrote, "I tremble for Philadelphia." The general was soon to learn how Philadelphia and the Congress would more than tremble when his alarming letters were received.

With little delay, Congress adjourned to reconvene on the 20th in Baltimore. Before they adjourned, they resolved "That, until Congress shall otherwise order, General Washington be possessed of full power to order and direct all things relative to the department, and the operations of the war." Reflecting the fear expressed by Congress, the road from Philadelphia to Baltimore soon was "full of the citizens of Philadelphia who had fled with their families and effects . . . by the thousands."

On the 11th, Gen. Washington sent Lieutenant Colonel John Nixon with Colonel John Cadwalader's regiment to Dunk's Ferry to guard that crossing. He also sent Captain Henry Miller of Colonel Edward Hand's Pennsylvania rifle regiment across the Delaware, near Bordentown, with a strong scouting party.

Upon Capt. Miller's return from his mission he reported that he fell in with about 400 Hessian troops "marching to Burlington." The troops fired upon him and he retreated across the river. This strong move to the south was confirmed by Com. Seymour, who patrolled the river up to Burlington on the 11th and reported that four or five hundred of the enemy had entered the town.

Based on Capt. Miller's and Com. Seymour's reports, Gen. Washington began to deploy the remainder of his force along the Delaware River to the south. Brigadier General Philemon Dickinson was to make his headquarters at Yardley's Ferry, with his front extending to a point two miles below Yardley's where Brigadier General James Ewing's sector began. Gen. Ewing's headquarters were to be near Hoop's Mill on Biles Creek where there was a ford over the Delaware at the upper end of the island near the mill. Gen. Ewing's front was to run to Kirkbride's or Bordentown Ferry, where Col. Cadwalader's front began. Col. Cadwalader was to make his headquarters at Bristol with his front extending to Dunk's Ferry at which place Gen. Washington recommended Lt. Col. Nixon's regiment be allowed to continue where it was.

Howe Rearranges Command

While Gen. Washington was busily engaged at his Pennsylvania headquarters, Gen. Howe was equally busy at his Trenton, New Jersey, headquarters across the river, about a mile away. After the failure of Cornwallis to cross the Delaware, because of the lack of boats, Howe ended the campaign and began to establish winter quarters for his army in New Jersey. It took four days to make the necessary arrangements, during which time the two sections of his army remained in bivouac outside of Trenton and Pennington, the next town north.

These were four restless days for Gen. Washington. Although the water of the Delaware had stopped Cornwallis, Washington was reminded that it could be only a temporary halt. The general was informed that any day the Delaware might freeze solid and permit the passage of the British over the ice. The river had frozen solid during many winters before, and it could happen in a very few hours with a drop in temperature. Gen. Howe's army, still in bivouac, gave evidence of some impending move.

While Gen. Washington worried, Gen. Howe spent much of his time at Trenton taking oaths of allegiance from those who sought protection of the Crown. The oath read in part, "I do hearby promise and declare, that I will remain in a peaceable obedience to his Majesty, and will not take up arms, in opposition to his authority." Many took the oath because they earnestly wished to do so, others merely to protect their property.

Probably there were as many reasons for taking the oath as there were individuals, but each cut deeply at the American morale. Washington learned of the considerable numbers seeking protection and wrote to the Congress, "the Enemy are daily gathering strength from the disaffected; this Strength like a Snow ball by rolling, will Increase, unless some means can be devised to check it."

Others in and about Trenton, not sympathetic to the British cause, banded themselves together in secret armed groups, without uniforms, and fell upon small British military parties and the homes of British sympathizers. To counteract this, Gen. Howe issued orders that "Small straggling Parties, not dressed like Soldiers . . . who presume to molest or fire upon Soldiers or peaceable Inhabitants of the Country, will be immediately hanged without Trial, as assassins."

While Howe was greeting the disaffected and providing for their protection, his army was making shifts in command preparatory to taking up winter quarters in New Jersey, mainly at Brunswick, Princeton, Trenton, and Bordentown. The recently promoted Lieutenant General Cornwallis had asked to be relieved temporarily of his post so he could return to England, and Maj. Gen. Grant was given the over-all command of British forces in New Jersey.

One important command problem to be solved was at Trenton and Bordentown. It had been decided that the von Donop brigade of Hessian grenadiers and the Rall brigade of Hessian fusiliers would cover the area from Princeton to Burlington, but the manner in which the cordon should be drawn was under discussion. Colonel Carl Emil Ulrich von Donop was called in on this consultation with Generals Howe and Grant. Col. von Donop suggested that "It would not be suitable to leave complete regiments there [at Trenton] because they would be too tired by continuous disturbance."

Von Donop also suggested that headquarters be established at Bordentown, and that troops be assigned out of there on a rotating basis to Burlington and Trenton. Gen. Howe agreed and von Donop was given the over-all command from Princeton to Burlington.

When Colonel Johann Gottlieb Rall heard of the plan, he protested a rotating service for Trenton. Rall wanted his whole brigade to take the post at Trenton, and wished to rotate the expected strenuous service from within his brigade. Col. von Donop interpreted this position by Col. Rall as "improper ambition."

Col. Rall went to Gen. Grant and asked if he would intercede with Gen. Howe in his behalf. Grant did reopen the subject with Howe, and Rall was allowed to keep his brigade

with him at Trenton, but the over-all command remained with von Donop.

On December 14 both Col. Rall and Col. von Donop were in Trenton. Before departing for Bordentown, Col. von Donop wrote to Col. Rall transmitting Gen. Howe's orders and some instructions of his own. Von Donop ordered Rall to extend his guard posts as far south as Crosswicks Creek drawbridge, two and a half miles north of Bordentown, and to provide von Donop with a report in "the usual form every fourteen days."

Von Donop also showed Rall where he thought redoubts would be of use, and assigned Captain George Heinrich Pauli, an engineering officer with the Hessian troops, to lay out the redoubts before coming on to Bordentown to perform the same service there. The two sites selected at Trenton were on "the high ground on Pennington Road, [near the battle monument] and on the other side of the [Assunpink] bridge."

After attending to command affairs in this way Col. von Donop left Trenton on the 14th with his brigade, enroute to Bordentown. From the record, it does not appear that von Donop visited Ral! or that Rall visited von Donop during the next 12 days. (See Appendix C for military background of Rall and von Donop)

CHAPTER THREE

WINTER QUARTERS

Lee is Captured

On December 14, the day the British army came off bivouac to go into winter quarters, their camps at Trenton and Pennington were alive with excitement. The second ranking general of the United States army, Major General Charles Lee, had been captured at Basking Ridge and brought to Pennington.

TRENTON DURING THE REVOLUTION *This is an 18th century picture of a part of Trenton. It is a wood engraving published in the May 1789 issue of the Columbia Magazine. It is a view looking east. It shows General Washington entering the town of Trenton April 21, 1789 (some 12 years after the Battle of Trenton), enroute to New York where nine days later, on April 30, 1789, George Washington was inaugurated the first President of the United States of America. Washington can be seen on a white horse, approaching the Assunpink bridge from the south, and about to pass under the Triumphal Arch built for his reception. A portion of this arch has been preserved and is on display in the Old Barracks at Trenton.*

It happened this way. Gen. Lee had been slow in his march across New Jersey. He had crossed the North River at Peekskill on December 2, and in spite of Gen. Washington's urgent requests to join him, he had advanced no farther than Morristown by the 8th. In a letter to Washington on that date Lee said, "I can not persuade myself that Philadelphia is their object at present . . . It will be difficult, I am afraid, to join you; but cannot I do you more service by attacking their rear?"

The British were very concerned about Lee being on their flank. An army of 2000, which Gen. Howe thought to be about 3000, could be dangerous should it strike a sudden blow. Frequent British patrols were sent out to gain intelligence on Lee's corps.

It was one of these patrols dispatched by Gen. Cornwallis from Pennington, which luckily accomplished a task it had not set out to do. This patrol consisted of 30 dragoons from the 16th regiment, of Lieutenant Colonel William Harcourt.

On the 12th, while scouting the area of upper Somerset County, Harcourt learned that Gen. Lee was quartered at Basking Ridge, "in one White's house," some distance outside his main camp. Early in the morning of the 13th, Harcourt and his men rode almost to the door of Lee's headquarters, "undiscovered by the guard, surrounded it, and overcame all resistance, and made the General prisoner." Two of Lee's aides were killed and "He himself requested his Life Might be spared, and was brought to Penny Town [Pennington] on the 14th."

Not knowing that Lee had been captured, Washington wrote to Lee on the 14th, "I have so frequently mentioned our Situation, and the necessity of your Aid, that it is painful to me to add a Word upon the subject."

After his capture, Lee's command fell to Major General John Sullivan. It was Gen. Sullivan who got the first word to Gen. Washington. Although Sullivan sent the message on the 13th, Washington did not receive it until the 15th. Washington promptly sent a message to Sullivan simply referring him to the several letters written to Lee, and adding his regrets at the unhappy fate of Lee.

On the 14th, the day after Gen. Lee's capture, Gen. Howe issued the following orders: "The Campaign having closed with the Pursuit of the Enemies' Army near, ninety Miles, by Lieut. Gen. Cornwallis Corps . . . The Approach of Winter putting a Stop to any further Progress, The Troops will immediately march into Quarters and hold themselves in Readiness to assemble on the shortest Notice."

Gen. Howe left Trenton on the 14th and probably went to Pennington, where Gen. Lee was being held, then to Brunswick, from which place on the 17th he and Gen. Cornwallis departed for New York.

The 14th was a busy day, and most of the British army in New Jersey was in motion. Col. Rall's brigade moved into Trenton and the von Donop brigade marched to Bordentown. Brigadier General Alexander Leslie took up quarters in Princeton, with the 2nd brigade, two battalions of light infantry, and three troops of the 16th dragoons. Maj. Gen. Grant established command headquarters at Brunswick with the 1st and 2nd battalions of British grenadiers and three troops of the 16th dragoons. The 4th brigade, also attached to headquarters, was housed along the road from Brunswick to Bushwick (now Middleboro) some as far out as Hillsborough (now Millstone). Brigadier

OLD BARRACKS AT TRENTON *This U-shaped building of native undressed stone was built in 1758, during the French and Indian War, to quarter troops stationed at, or passing through, Trenton so they would not have to be quartered in homes. The building is two stories high with cellar. The main building is 130 X 18½ feet, with wings of 58 feet on each end. Soon after completion, a two and a half story addition was added to house commissioned officers. This addition is the present entrance building to the Old Barracks Association's museum. The building is located at Willow and West Front Streets, on the State House grounds.*

General Edward Matthew, with the two battalions of Guards, made his headquarters just across the river from Brunswick at Raritan Landing. Gen. Matthew was put in charge of outposts at Amboy, Spank Town (now Carteret), Elizabethtown, Newark, Acquackanonk (now Passaic), Powles Hook and Bergen (both now Jersey City).

The chain of command in New Jersey was as follows: Maj. Gen. Grant was field commander, with Brig. Gen. Leslie, Brig. Gen. Matthew, and Col. von Donop reporting directly to him. Col. von Donop was to communicate with Brig. Gen. Leslie at Princeton but was not ordinarily expected to take orders from him. Col. Rall was to report directly to Col. von Donop at Bordentown.

In the American camp on the 14th it was also moving day of sorts. Gen. Washington on that day moved his headquarters from Thomas Barclay's house, opposite Trenton, to William Keith's house about 10 miles farther north. This was done so the general could be "near the main body of my army." Keith's house was located on Jericho Creek, as the road runs, about two and a half miles in from the Delaware, southwest of Brownsburg. Major Generals Nathaniel Greene and John Sullivan were already located less than a half mile from Keith's. Colonel Henry Knox, in charge of artillery, was a little over a mile away, and Brigadier General Stirling, in charge of river defenses in that sector, made his headquarters in the Thompson-Neely house on the Delaware, about three and a half miles from Keith's.

Militia Annoys von Donop

No sooner had Gen. Howe ordered his troops into winter quarters than Gen. Washington started laying plans to attack Howe's extended line across New Jersey's middle. On the 14th,

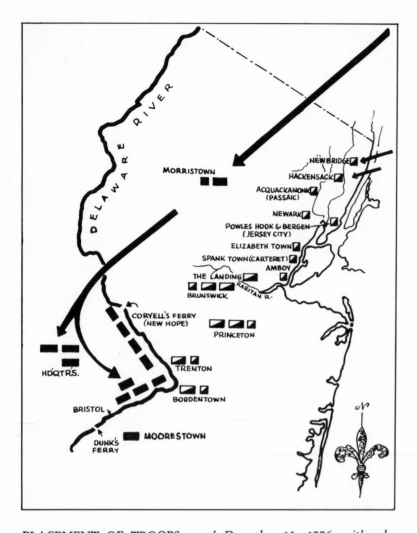

PLACEMENT OF TROOPS *as of December 15, 1776, with subsequent assignments to December 25 indicated by arrows.*
AMERICAN *brigades and detachments were deployed in Pennsylvania between Coryell's Ferry and Dunk's Ferry as follows: Above the elbow of the Delaware, from north to south, were the brigades of Col. Haussegger, Brig. Gen. Stirling, Brig. Gen. Stephen, Brig. Gen. Mercer, and a force of about 500 New Jersey militia under Brig. Gen. Dickinson. This northern sector was reinforced on December 22 by the arrival at headquarters of the brigades of Col. Sargent, Col. Glover, Brig. Gen. St. Clair and Col. Hitchcock. In the crook of the elbow and below it, from north to south, were the brigades of Brig. Gen. Ewing and Col. Cadwalader. This southern sector was reinforced on December 23 by Col. Hitchcock's brigade from headquarters. In northern New Jersey, at Morristown, were three regiments under Lt. Col. Vose and 200 New Jersey militia under Col. Ford. In southern New Jersey, at Moorestown, were 500 New Jersey militia under the command of Col. Griffin.*
BRITISH *brigades and detachments were deployed in New Jersey as follows: south of the Raritan River at Brunswick and vicinity under Maj. Gen. Grant, 4th brigade, British grenadiers (2 battalions), 16th dragoons (3 troops); at Princeton under Brig. Gen. Leslie, 2nd brigade, light infantry (2 battalions), 16th dragoons (3 troops); at Trenton under Col. Rall, Rall brigade Hessian fusiliers, Hessian Jaegers (50 men), 16th dragoons (20 men); at Bordentown and vicinity under Col. von Donop, von Donop brigade of Hessian grenadiers, 42nd regiment (2 battalions), Hessian Jaegers (2 companies). Deployed north of the Raritan River, all under Brig. Gen. Matthew with headquarters at The Landing, were units as follows: at The Landing, Guards brigade; Amboy, 33rd regiment; Spank Town, 46th regiment, 17th dragoons (1 troop); Elizabeth Town, Waldeck regiment, 17th dragoons (1 troop); Powles Hook, 57th regiment (50 men); Bergen, 57th regiment (balance of men); Newark, 71st regiment (2 battalions); Acquackanonk, 71st regiment (1 battalion). As of December 21, additional troops were stationed at: Hackensack, 26th regiment; New Bridge, 7th regiment. (For breakdown of American and British Brigades by regiment, see Appendix A).*

Gen. Washington wrote Governor Jonathan Trumbull of Massachusetts that as soon as the northern army of Major Generals Charles Lee and Horatio Gates, amounting to about 2600 effective troops, should arrive, he hoped "to attempt a Stroke upon the Forces of the Enemy, who lay a good deal scattered and to all appearance in a state of Security. A lucky Blow in this Quarter, would be fatal to them, and would most certainly raise the Spirits of the People, which are quite sunk by our late misfortunes."

Washington probably had not yet determined where he would strike, but certainly he planned some action to be taken before the end of the year, at which time expiring enlistments would again reduce his force, this time to "Fourteen or Fifteen hundred effective Men."

During the period of time Washington had to wait for Gens. Sullivan and Gates to arrive in camp, there was one large imponderable facing the general. Would the British be able to cross the river on the ice (or in boats they might bring up or construct) before he could launch an offensive of his own?

Washington knew how far troops could march in a day and surely he was able to predict that Sullivan and Gates could not possibly arrive in camp until the 20th or 21st. Thus, during this week, Washington planned to annoy the enemy with raids and, under the cover of these raids, send spies over to New Jersey to gather as much intelligence as possible.

To this end Washington wrote to his general officers as follows: "Let me entreat you to cast about to find out some Person who can be engaged to cross the River as a spy . . . particularly enquiry to be made by the person sent if any preparations are making to cross the River."

To accomplish his plan of gathering information and harassment, until he was prepared to fight, Gen. Washington relied mainly on the New Jersey and the Pennsylvania militia, plus the Pennsylvania state navy. The first annoyance was to be against Col. von Donop at Bordentown.

Von Donop had arrived at Bordentown on the 14th, with three Hessian grenadier battalions: Block, von Linsing and von Minnigerode. To his command had been added the 42nd regiment, or the Scottish "Black Watch" plus two Jaeger rifle companies, one of them temporarily mounted. Von Donop's force numbered about 1500 men.

The town of Bordentown was found to be so small that the 42nd regiment and the Block battalion had to be quartered in and near Black Horse, now Columbus. The von Minnigerode and von Linsing battalions were placed in about 20 houses in Bordentown proper. Conditions were crowded beyond reason, and to remedy this, on the morning of the 15th, von Donop ordered the von Linsing battalion to move out of town into farmhouses in and around Sun Tavern, now Mansfield Square, with battalion headquarters in the tavern. The troops were in the middle of moving when the first of a long series of incidents occurred, aimed at keeping the Hessians off balance at Trenton and Bordentown.

To von Donop's surprise, two armed gondolas of the Pennsylvania navy had come up the Delaware to Bordentown and anchored above the town. Col. von Donop took the two English six pounders he had with him and placed them overlooking the river. He was about to fire when the Americans saw the operation and hastily withdrew down the river.

Von Donop had hoped to occupy Burlington, 10 miles below Bordentown, but now he realized that its position close to the river on low ground made it vulnerable to gunfire from the Pennsylvania navy gondolas. Von Donop was therefore forced to delay the permanent occupation of Burlington until he should be able to drive off the gondolas with the six 18 pounders scheduled to arrive soon with the fourth Hessian grenadier battalion, Koehler.

As night fell on the 15th, von Donop had all of his troops quartered, although quite spread out. The two Jaeger companies covered the flanks as follows: a Jaeger detachment was posted near Crosswicks Creek, south of the drawbridge; another was posted on the Delaware, near "Miss Whitfield's house," now Fieldsboro; a third Jaeger detachment was posted at "Lewis' Mill" on Black Creek, just south of Bordentown. The mounted Jaegers were assigned to no special place; they were to cover from Crosswicks to New Mill, now Pemberton, to secure the back country and bring in forage and necessary food to Bordentown.

Jersey Militia Attack

On the 16th, Col. von Donop received the report that a large American force was marching from Philadelphia up through New Jersey. Von Donop sent 200 grenadiers and the mounted Jaegers to Mount Holly to investigate. The strong Hessian scouting party went as far as Moorestown, where they found some case-shot balls near the bridge, but no enemy. After throwing the shot into the water of the North Branch of Pensauken Creek, the party returned.

The American force, which had withdrawn from Moorestown, was five New Jersey militia regiments from Cumberland, Gloucester and Salem Counties, and two Virginia artillery companies with two 3 pounders. Their strength was approximately 500 men. These troops, under the command of Colonel Samuel Griffin, advanced and retreated, advanced and retreated, keeping von Donop off guard.

On the 19th, Col. von Donop and Col. Block personally reconnoitered the area with a large party, going as far south as Mount Holly. Here they sent out a small detachment which found the bridge over the Rancocas destroyed. This halted their push forward, and caused the Hessians again to return to their bases.

On the 22nd there was another incident. At 2 p.m. in the afternoon, the alarm cannon at Sun Tavern was fired, and was heard by von Donop in Bordentown. Von Donop answered the alarm, picking up the von Linsing battalion as he went through Sun Tavern, and hastening to Black Horse, where he learned that there had been a skirmish with the enemy at Slabtown, now Jacksonville.

An American eyewitness account of this attack by Col. Griffin and his New Jersey militia stated that "the enemy were forced to retreat with precipitation, having some killed, and leaving behind them many knapsacks and other necessaries, amongst which was a hat shot through the crown."

By the time von Donop had the full report, it was becoming dark. A bivouac was ordered at Slabtown, and the next morning the Scottish 42nd regiment and the Block battalion marched directly to Mount Holly. The von Linsing battalion marched to Mt. Holly over a longer route, via the bridge across Assiscunk Creek, about a mile southwest of Bustleton. At this point they picked up the 2nd Jaeger company, which had been sent there to protect the bridge.

THOMPSON-NEELY HOUSE *This lovely 18th century home, now a museum and furnished in contemporary style, was the headquarters of Brig. Gen. Lord Stirling (William Alexander) beginning December 9, 1776; and it was from near this house that the general marched his men to Mc Konkey's Ferry the afternoon of December 25, preparatory to the attack on Trenton.*

As von Donop approached Mount Holly over the direct route, he was met by about 100 of the enemy posted on the hill near the church. There was some cannon fire from the Americans, but only momentarily. They soon limbered their guns and withdrew through Mount Holly toward Moorestown. During the two day skirmish the New Jersey militia lost "two killed and seven or eight wounded."

On the 24th, all being quiet, the von Linsing battalion marched back to their quarters in farmhouses around Sun Tavern. Col. von Donop stayed in Mount Holly with the 42nd regiment and the Block battalion, plus the Jaegers, to collect forage and food in the neighborhood and to "let those longing for protection, take the oath of honor to the King."

CHAPTER FOUR

RALL HARASSED

From the South

While Col. von Donop was being attacked on the southern sector during the week of December 15 through 22, Col. Rall also was being harassed at Trenton.

His brigade had moved out of bivouac at Pennington on the 14th, and into houses in Trenton. In addition to the three regiments of his brigade, Rall, von Lossberg and von Knyphausen, Col. Rall was assigned "50 [Hessian] Jaegers and 20 [British] dragoons," the latter from the 16th regiment, to be used mainly for carrying messages and some long distance patrol work. The dragoons were to be relieved once a week from Princeton.

The four companies of the Rall regiment were assigned to houses on the southern and middle portions of what is now

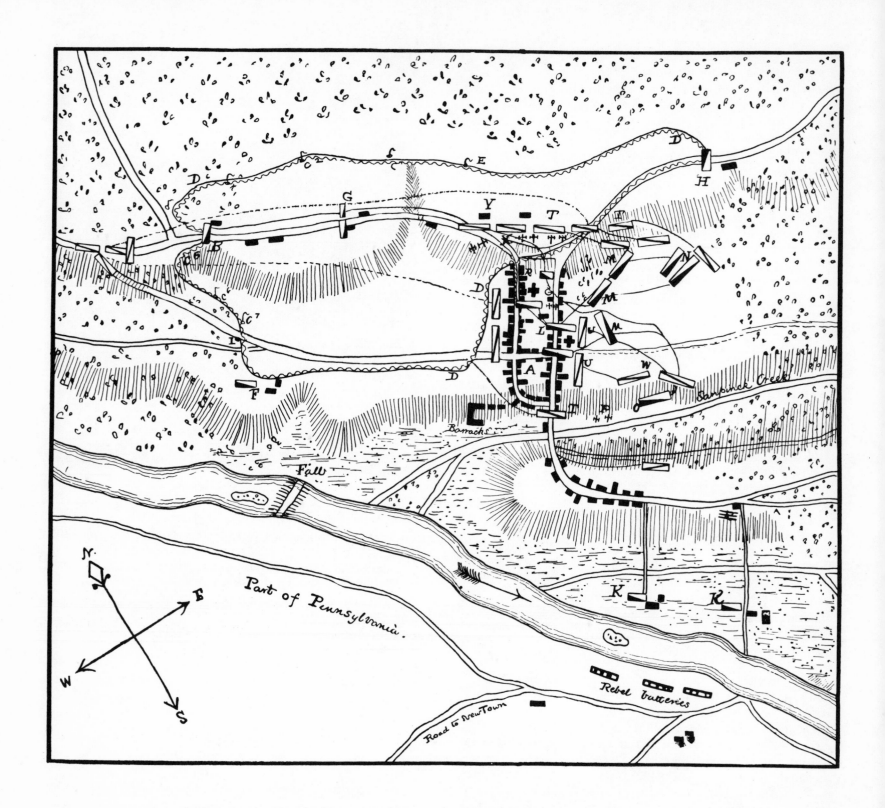

PIEL MAP OF TRENTON   *This map by Lieutenant Jacob Piel, Hessian brigade adjutant, is in the State Archives, Marburg, Germany.   It was prepared in 1778 or 1779 and constituted one of the exhibits at the Hessian war trials. Map explanation follows: A. Trenton. B. Picket of 1 officer and 24 men.   C. The 7 picket posts placed on each side of it; No. 1 was the right wing, and had connection with the left wing of the captain's picket; No. 7 was the left wing, and had connection with the Jaeger picket. D. Route made by the patrol of captain's picket, which turned to the left at the Jaeger picket and proceeded uptown to the captain's post, thence back through the chain of sentinels. E. The left wing of the captain's picket. F. Right wing of the Jaeger picket. G. Captain von Altenbockum's company of the von Lossberg regiment.   H. Picket consisting of 1 captain, 1 non-commissioned officer and 75 men. I. Picket of 1 officer and 50 Jaegers. K. Command of 1 officer and 30 men. L. Where the Rall and von Lossberg regiments formed and received orders. M. Place where regiments tried to rally. N. Place to which regiments Rall and von Lossberg were driven and surrendered. O. Place where von Knyphausen regiment surrendered. P. Von Lossberg cannon in swamp. Q. Von Knyphausen cannon. R. Rall cannon. S. Attack of Americans from woods. T. Junction of Americans before the city. U. Stirling's brigade which pursued the von Knyphausen regiment. W. Last movement of Americans. X. American cannon. Y. Place from which General Washington directed the battle.*

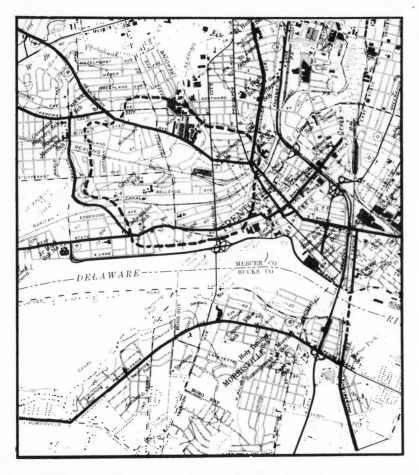

PIEL MAP INTERPRETATION *The Lt. Jacob Piel map of 1778 or 1779 is projected onto a 1957 U. S. Department of Interior Geological Survey Map showing approximate troop movements in relation to modern points of reference.*

North Warren Street. Col. Rall selected for his brigade headquarters a house on the west side of the street across from the English Church, now Perry and North Warren.

The Hessians, in their records and diaries, continuously refer to North Warren as "high street" (the British equivalent of Main Street) and to North Broad as "bridge street" (meaning the street leading to the bridge), using no other designations for streets in Trenton.

The four companies of the von Knyphausen regiment occupied almost the whole of Bridge Street. The von Lossberg regiment, having been on temporary duty at Elizabethtown until replaced by the Waldeck regiment, was therefore the last of the Rall regiments to arrive in Trenton. By then, most of the suitable houses in town had been taken, and the four companies of the von Lossberg regiment had to be quartered at first in houses much stretched out, along the Pennington Road. This was soon corrected and only one company of the four, that of Captain Ernst von Altenbockum, remained in two houses on the Pennington Road. The other three companies found quarters on the north end of High Street.

When the Rall force was fully assembled in Trenton it numbered 1586 officers and men, as closely as can be determined. (See Appendix D)

Immediately upon his arrival in town, Col. Rall established patrol stations to keep his lines of communication open to Bordentown on the south and Princeton on the north. The Bordentown Road patrol station was headquartered at the Crosswicks drawbridge, and consisted of 100 men and one captain, to be rotated every 48 hours. The Princeton Road

patrol station, which was rotated daily, consisted of one captain, one noncommissioned officer and 70 to 75 men, with headquarters near Trenton on the Princeton Road.

Small picket posts were established at other locations. One was placed in a house on Pennington Road just east of the junction with what is now Parkway Avenue. The Jaegers, who were expert riflemen, held down the river posts. One detachment was placed above the town and housed in the home of Gen. Dickinson located between River Road and the Delaware on what is now Colonial Avenue, and called "The Hermitage." The other was quartered in the ferry house below town at the foot of Ferry Street.

December 14, 15 and 16 were quiet in Trenton. Then on the 17th, the day after the 20 light dragoons arrived from Princeton for duty, they were sent on patrol to Pennington where one of them was "deadly wounded" by one of Gen. Dickinson's scouting parties.

That same morning, Gen. Ewing's Pennsylvania militia began a "strong cannonade and under the cover of the fire, some 30 or more men were landed" at the ferry picket post south of Trenton. Before Rall could bring up reinforcements, Ewing's men withdrew across the river. The picket at the ferry had been one officer and six Jaegers but after the attack Rall supplemented the post with six additional Jaegers and supported it with an officer and 30 infantrymen stationed nearby, at Dr. William Bryant's house, formerly the home of William Trent.

On the 18th, the Jaeger detachment at the ferry was attacked again at dawn, under a barrage of "18 cannon shot," causing the Jaegers to retire out of range. As before, the landing party, estimated at about 50 men, quickly returned to the other side.

After the second attack at the ferry, Col. Rall ordered that every morning before daybreak the staff officer of the day with about 70 men and two cannon proceed to the lower ferry, and remain there behind the hill until 10 a.m., prepared for another attack.

From the North

While the second attack at the ferry was in progress, Col. Rall received an urgent message that a small American unit had landed "four miles above Trenton at Howel's Ferry." Rall sent 12 Jaegers on foot from the post at The Hermitage, plus two dragoons, to investigate. One dragoon was killed in the skirmish with an estimated "rebel unit of 100 men" belonging to Dickinson's New Jersey militia force. Rall immediately sent out a large force "of 220 men" to destroy the scouting party but Dickinson's men, who lived in the neighborhood, seemed to disappear into the countryside.

On the 19th, Rall had additional losses when a Dickinson scouting party "captured three men of the von Lossberg regiment who went out to procure forage two miles from here [Trenton] not far from the road to Maidenhead."

From the moment Col. Rall entered Trenton, Gen. Dickinson's New Jersey militia occupied and controlled, almost at will, the area near Howell's Ferry on the New Jersey side of the Delaware. Rall and von Donop even identified one force near Howell's Ferry as that of "Colonel [David] Chambers of Hunterdon County . . . with 70 or 80 men."

On the 20th, Lieutenant Friedrich von Grothausen went on patrol "up the Delaware four miles" to Howell's Ferry, with

20 of his Jaegers from The Hermitage, plus four dragoons. At the ferry von Grothausen "met a rebel detachment of 150 men," and had a skirmish. Von Grothausen captured one American and reported one dragoon's mount killed. The identity of this American attacking unit is revealed in a letter to Gen. Washington on the 21st. Gen. Dickinson wrote from his headquarters at "Yardley's Farm," nearly across the river from Howell's, that "Captain Anderson, with his party returned yesterday, with the loss of one man taken, and two or three missing. The snow hastened his return."

In another mission on the 20th, Col. Rall sent two dragoons to Princeton with letters. They had been out for almost an hour when one dragoon returned to report that his companion had been killed from ambush. Rall then sent one captain and a hundred men with one piece of artillery to deliver the letters. One letter was a request from Col. Rall to Gen. Leslie asking that 200 men be stationed at Maidenhead to keep open lines of communication, and to do patrol work over to Howell's and Johnson's Ferries. Rall was criticized by Leslie for his extravagant use of manpower and was denied the request for support at Maidenhead.

During Rall's entire stay at Trenton, Howell's and Johnson's Ferries "were not held" by the Hessians. This presented a constant threat to the troops in Trenton.

After several attacks by Gen. Dickinson's militia, Major Justus Matthaeus of the Rall regiment appealed to Col. Rall, suggesting that it was "necessary for Pennington to be held by a detachment from which there could be detailed scouts to John's [Johnson's] ferry and in this manner they could watch the movements of the enemy." Rall replied, "What if the detachment should be lost and would the major like to be sent there?" The major answered that he would go if ordered, but Rall thought it too dangerous, unless it was a force of at least 200 men, which he could not afford.

It appears that the militia attacks from the north and south by Generals Dickinson and Ewing were not planned and scheduled; rather it was left to each commander to determine the appropriate time to launch a harassing movement or to cover a spy crossing. It is also evident that the attacking party had the privilege of staying across on the New Jersey side, returning whenever they thought it expedient. Since most of Dickinson's and some of Ewing's force lived in the area, they knew every hiding place.

Rall Wants Help

While Col. Rall was in the process of asking for a force from Gen. Leslie, to be quartered at Maidenhead, Col. von Donop was dispatching a request to Rall for the loan of one of Rall's regiments to do temporary duty with von Donop. Von Donop had information that Col. Griffin's force south of Bordentown had grown to "4000 of the enemy" and he planned to march against them. He needed his entire force for the task, plus one of Rall's regiments to watch stores in Bordentown and vicinity.

Rall replied, "It is impossible, my brother, to spare a battalion of my brigade as I am liable to be attacked at any moment. I have the enemy before me, behind me and on my right flank . . . I have not made any redoubts or any kind of fortifications because I have the enemy in all directions." Rall pleaded with von Donop that instead he should be relieved of the distant post near Bordentown at Crosswicks Creek drawbridge. Soldier that he was, Rall ended his letter to von Donop with, "I am ready to obey my brother" should this be his final decision.

Col. Rall seemed to be making no progress with his appeals to Leslie and von Donop; therefore on the 20th, Rall went over their heads and addressed "three letters" to Gen. Grant at Brunswick. He wrote of the "fatigue and alarm" of his brigade and repeated his request for support at Maidenhead. Some had not "had their cartridge pouches off for eight days." The next day Col. Rall received a letter from Gen. Grant refusing to place a detachment at Maidenhead and ridiculing the American force by describing them as having neither shoes nor stockings and being "in fact almost naked, dying and cold, without blankets and very ill supplied with Provisions." A copy of Grant's letter was sent to von Donop.

While waiting to hear from Gen. Grant, Col. Rall wrote to Gen. Leslie informing him of Col. von Donop's request for the loan of a regiment. In response, Leslie sent the 1st Light Infantry battalion to Trenton and the 2nd Light Infantry battalion to Maidenhead on the 21st. However, when von Donop informed Rall that his regiment would not be needed, because the rumor of 4000 advancing rebels was unfounded, the British reinforcements returned to Princeton.

At Rall's headquarters, one crisis followed another. One officer entered in his diary "Sentries, Commands, and pickets

HESSIANS AT TRENTON *These 18th century prints show the officers' and enlisted mens' uniforms of all Hessian troops at the Battle of Trenton: the Rall regiment, the von Knyphausen regiment, the von Lossberg regiment and the Jaeger corps. These unique prints have never before been published. Colored transparencies of each, with descriptive material, are available from the publisher.*

no end, in spite of being of no use, only being a restless busyness around the Hn. Brigadier's quarters the whole day."

Col. von Donop's prophecy to Gen. Howe, a week earlier, that any troops stationed permanently at Trenton "would be too tired by continuous disturbance," had certainly come true.

CHAPTER FIVE

WASHINGTON'S WORRIES

Enlistments, Clothing, Ice

Even Washington's enemies knew the magnitude of his worries. A Hessian diary summarizes very well the manpower problems faced by Washington. The diarist wrote "The duty-time of General Ewing's brigade of 600 expires on January 1 . . . The New England or so called Jankees have declared the same to go home on January 1, the end of their enlistment time. The Jankees amount to the greater part of Washington's army. Four other regiments besides these were also told not to serve after January 1 in other than their own counties."

Regarding these "so called Jankees" Generals Sullivan and Gates had arrived in camp on the 20th ahead of their New England troops, numbering about 2600 men. Their report to Washington was that "few or no men are recruited [for re-enlistment] out of the regiments," all of whose enlistments were to expire January 1. The troops when they did arrive were described as "without Shoes or Blankets and otherwise in wretched Plight," one reason why they were reluctant to continue in service.

The new enlistments Washington had expected failed also to materialize, adding to his problems. In Philadelphia, Gen. Israel Putnam, who had been sent there to act as a funnel for troops coming up to the front, was forced to report as of 9 a.m. the 20th, that only the Dover militia company of less than 50 men had arrived in town and reported to Putnam for orders. Gen. Washington wrote to Governor Trumbull of Massachusetts, "When I reflect upon what our Situation in this Quarter will be, in ten days from this; I am almost led to despair."

To Congress, Washington wrote "The Cloathing of the Troops is a matter of infinite importance . . . Their distresses are extremely great, many of 'em being entirely naked and most so thinly clad as to be unfit for service."

On December 19, the Pennsylvania Journal printed Thomas Paine's stirring words, "These are the times that try men's souls." And at about the same time the Journal was being distributed, a severe snow storm began, covering much of Pennsylvania and New Jersey. The storm continued throughout the day, the night and the next day, and the weather was described as "very cold."

One blow upon another seemed to strike Gen. Washington. On the 21st, a letter was intercepted from a loyalist with Gen. Howe's forces to his business associate in Philadelphia. The letter declared that it was the plan of Howe's army to be in Philadelphia between December 16 and December 26, "as soon as the ice is made." After receipt of this piece of intelligence Washington wrote to Congress, "Had I entertained a doubt of General Howe's intentions to pass the Delaware . . . it would now be done away."

On the 23rd, after three days of extreme cold, the Delaware began to freeze. It was completely frozen over by day's end, "but it was not [hard] enough to cross on it." Washington was sure that time had run out on him and that the enemy would be across the ice in a matter of hours. Within 48 hours the weather did warm up and the ice broke, but Washington worried until it happened.

British Scout Countryside

Over the preceding few days, there had been several probes by British forces. On the 16th, Gen. Matthew with part of the brigade of Guards, left "The Landing" opposite Brunswick and marched to Pluckimin, where he fell in with a small body of Americans. One soldier and one civilian guide of Matthew's force were wounded.

On the 17th, Gen. Leslie with part of his Princeton force began a march to Springfield, Bound Brook and back to Princeton. At Springfield, Leslie had 3 men wounded, undoubtedly by New Jersey militia, and reported three Americans killed and several others wounded. On the same day Lieutenant Colonel Charles Mawhood with part of his 4th brigade marched from their quarters along the road from Brunswick to Hillsborough toward Flemington.

These moves were interpreted by Washington to be an attempt to capture the three eastern regiments coming down from Ticonderoga to join his forces, although he knew they might also be preparatory to a march on Philadelphia. These troops coming to join Washington under Lieutenant Colonel Joseph Vose, were Colonel John Greaton's, Colonel William Bond's and Colonel Elisha Porter's regiments. Their total strength was "between five and six hundred Men."

To prevent their capture, Washington was compelled to halt Vose's three regiments at Morristown and to send Brigadier General William Maxwell (then without a brigade, and whose home was in nearby Sussex County) to take command there. Already assembled at Morristown were "about 200 militia" from the northern counties of New Jersey, led by Colonel Jacob Ford.

Then, what seemed to be a final blow was struck against Washington's attempt to launch an offensive ahead of the British. Maj. Gen. Gates, a field officer of great experience, was taken ill and departed for Philadelphia.

Gen. Washington's week of December 16 through 23 was surely one to "try men's souls."

CHAPTER SIX

ATTACK PLANNED

Secrecy The Word

On December 22, Colonel Joseph Reed, Washington's adjutant general, wrote to Gen. Washington from Col. Cadwalader's headquarters at Bristol, stating that Col. Griffin had advanced with his 600 New Jersey militia and Virginia artillery "as far as Mount Holly within seven miles of their [Hessian] headquarters at Black Horse." Col. Griffin feared to advance farther with such a small force, and wrote to Col. Cadwalader for two pieces of artillery and two or three hundred volunteers to strengthen his corps. Instead, Cols. Cadwalader and Reed suggested to Gen. Washington that Cadwalader's force of about 1500 Pennsylvania militia be allowed to cross the river the next morning, the 23rd, to support Griffin in an attack on Black Horse.

Washington immediately informed Col. Griffin that other plans were in the making and that Griffin and Cadwalader should not go ahead with their suggested crossing. This was repeated in a letter to Griffin on the 23rd, advising him to go to Bristol and stay there two or three days, to coordinate matters with Cadwalader on the plan, which Washington wrote, "I hinted to you as having in mind here."

The plan referred to was the outgrowth of a statement by Gen. Washington to Gov. Trumbull of Massachusetts nine days earlier, that as soon as Generals Gates' and Lee's forces should arrive in camp he hoped to "attempt a stroke upon the Forces of the Enemy."

To Col. Cadwalader, Gen. Washington hurried off a dispatch which arrived at Cadwalader's headquarters "at 9 o'clock" a.m. on the 23rd. Washington informed Cadwalader that he "had determined on his plan of attacking the British posts on Christmas night, and would not have any of the troops harassed in the meantime." In this letter to Cadwalader Washington still withheld details of the attack, stating that "he would send his plan in a day or two."

This appears to be the first mention in writing of the date of attack, and followed a meeting on the evening before, the 22nd, attended by Generals "Sullivan, Gates, Arnold, and Stirling," plus of course Washington.

On the 24th, Washington sent Cadwalader full particulars regarding the plan against Trenton and told him to "fix with Col. Griffin on our Points of Attack . . . but let the hour of attack be on the 26th, and one hour before day (of that morning)." This information was in Cadwalader's hands the morning of the 24th, and he then "privately communicated all of the important information" to Captain Thomas Rodney, whose company of Dover, Kent County, Delaware militia, on that day became officially joined to Cadwalader's brigade.

To support Col. Cadwalader in the southern sector, Washington sent down to Bristol Colonel Daniel Hitchcock's New England brigade, numbering about 500 to 600 men. Washington was aware that because "some of the Continental Colonels have gone down with the brigade . . . [Cadwalader being a militia colonel] I fear there may be some uneasiness about command there." Washington felt obliged, therefore, to arrange the promotion of Col. Cadwalader to the rank of brigadier general of militia, in order to avoid that uneasiness.

For the attack, Cadwalader was ordered to provide his men with blankets and cooked provisions for three days. Fortunately, a supply of blankets had been sent up from Philadelphia a day or two earlier. Washington hoped Cadwalader would cross the Delaware near Bristol at the appointed hour, and together with Griffin "move forward if possible, so as to form a junction with me."

Washington also had some hope that Gen. Putnam could move across the Delaware from Philadelphia with new troops that were assembling there. To expedite this action, on the night of the 24th, Col. Reed went to Philadelphia to urge Gen. Putnam, if possible, to reinforce Col. Griffin. This was very short notice, but it was hoped that Putnam would at least be able to form a reserve, should something unexpected materialize on the southern sector. Reed learned from Putnam that "the shortness of time and the unprovided state of the

militia did not admit of the corporation design." Thus, after resting a few hours, Col. Reed "returned to Bristol."

Gen. Washington's plan for a strong attack from Col. Griffin's force was dampened further when it was learned that Col. Griffin's illness, which had been coming on for the past few days, had now put him out of action, forcing him to go to Philadelphia for medical attention. "The two companies of Virginians had also returned, leaving their two small Pieces of Iron Cannon and a few militia at Morris Town [Moorestown] and Haddonfield." After Col. Griffin's departure, his force was led by Colonel Silas Newcomb of the Cumberland County, New Jersey, militia.

To the north of Gen. Cadwalader, Gen. Ewing made his plans to move over the river at Trenton Ferry just below the town, with a force of about "600 men," all drawn from the Pennsylvania militia. The strategy was that Gen. Ewing would seize "the [Assunpink] bridge leading out of town." Gen. Dickinson, who, for the preceding week had controlled the area around Howell's Ferry from his post at Yardley's, appears to have continued in this assignment.

Gen. Washington was to lead all the forces north of Gen. Dickinson's post. These were the troops to be used in the main assault on Trenton from the north, at dawn on the 26th.

Gen. Washington's force which was to cross at McKonkey's Ferry was "about 2400" men and, with the exception of the Pennsylvania German regiment under Col. Haussegger and one other small unit, the entire corps had been with Washington in all or part of his retreat across New Jersey.

The other new unit which had been added to Washington's force was the 1st troop of Philadelphia cavalry. This small troop and the few of Sheldon's dragoons not carrying messages, were the only cavalry which Washington had available.

British-Hessian Complacency

While Gen. Washington was making last minute preparations, British and Hessian camps seemed to be unaware of the activity. On the 23rd, Gen. Grant wrote to Col. von Donop

MC KONKEY'S FERRY HOUSE OR OLD FERRY INN *It was in the old part of this ferry house that about two dozen Hessian officers spent the night of December 26, standing in one small room. The building, now somewhat enlarged, is of native stone construction, and stands close to the river bank on the north side of Pennsylvania state highway #532.*

that the 4th, or Koehler, battalion of grenadiers with the heavy artillery, had arrived at Amboy and were on their way to join von Donop. Grant added the comment "We are in great favor at home" for having driven Washington out of New Jersey. In a further display of unawareness of the coming attack, Col. von Donop spent the day before Christmas taking oaths of allegiance to the King, in Mount Holly.

On Christmas eve, however, Gen. Grant received intelligence that there was a planned attack on Trenton. "At past 11 at night" Christmas Eve, Grant hurried off a letter to von Donop with a copy to Rall (and probably one to Leslie) telling them that Washington had held a high level meeting "sunday last," the 22nd. At this meeting, Washington and his staff had discussed the fact that the British were "weak at Trenton and Princetown and Lord Stirling [Brig. Gen. Stirling] expressed a wish to make an attack upon these two places." Grant continued in his letter "I do not believe he will attempt it, but be assured that my information is undoubtedly true, so I need not advise you to be upon your guard."

Upon receipt of Grant's letter, Major Friedrich von Dechow urged Col. Rall to "send away the baggage, as it was only an encumbrance in case of an attack," but Rall did nothing about it, falling in with Gen. Grant's attitude, "I do not believe he will attempt it."

CHAPTER SEVEN

CHRISTMAS DAY

No Special Holiday

In America and in Britain, Christmas is celebrated on December 25, but in Germany Christmas extends over a two-day period, the 25th and 26th. These are the first and second days of Christmas. With the exception of a few additional minor details, Christmas customs and behavior in these three predominantly Christian countries were in 1776, and are today, quite similar.

In the British, German and American camps on December 25, which was a Wednesday, some of the men participated in special Christmas services held by the chaplains. During the day some exchanged gifts, and in the German quarters at Trenton, the familiar tannenbaum (the German Christmas tree) was in evidence. The Christmas tree custom had not yet come to America and Britain.

There is no on-the-scene evidence that there was any widespread drinking or celebrating in British, American or German camps on December 25 or 26. In the main, the troops were fearful, hungry, poorly clad, cold, and worried that they might never see another Christmas.

In Trenton, on Christmas morning, there was some snow on the ground but the temperature had risen over the past 24 hours to just below freezing. Parade and inspection were held at 11 a.m. Christmas morning. All men fit for duty were on the line except those on guard duty or on other special assignments. At 2 p.m., on schedule, the guard detail was changed. Col. Rall took part in the ceremonies, as he always did, standing before his quarters as the guard detail of about 200 men passed in review. The brigade band marched with the changing of the guard, and two cannon were paraded, as was the daily custom.

Maj. von Dechow of the Knyphausen regiment was the incoming officer of the day or "staff officer of the day" as he was called. Following the guard-changing ceremonies, Maj. von Dechow took up his headquarters for the 24 hour period in the guard house, located "50 paces" from Rall's headquarters. By 4 p.m. the outlying picket posts surrounding the town had been changed, and the old picket detail was back at the guard house ready to be dismissed.

The guard "duty was mixed;" that is, not all the men were drawn from the same regiment. Captain Johann Bruebach of the Rall regiment was incoming inspector of the guard, called "Captain of Inspection." Capt. Bruebach made his headquarters at the guard station on the Trenton-Princeton Road.

In addition to the guard detail there was another principal duty assignment. On the 25th, the Rall regiment, on a rotating basis, became the regiment of the day called the "de jour regiment." This meant that the regiment would sleep fully clothed Christmas night, so as to be quick to respond to any attack which might come in the night.

At dusk, the four companies of the Rall regiment marched to the three large buildings located in the lower part of town, designated "alarm houses." Guns were stacked out in front under guard, and the men filed in for the night. Lieutenant Colonel Balthasar Brethauer, senior officer of the Rall regiment, was with his troops.

The artillery detachments assigned to each regiment were not quartered with individual regiments but lived together in one house not far from the guard house. The cannon crew for the de jour regiment, however, did sleep fully dressed in their own quarters. All six brass "three pounder" cannon assigned to the Rall brigade (two to each regiment) stood one behind the other in front of the guard house. All artillery horses were kept in one barn not far from the crew's quarters and not far from the guard house. None of the artillery horses were unharnessed day or night, except to be groomed.

A Small Skirmish

"At 8 o'clock in the evening," as the men of the Rall regiment were settling down to rest as best they could, shots were heard above the town and there was great excitement. In moments, the Rall regiment was forming in front of the alarm houses. Other soldiers soon came out into the street to inquire what had happened, and the news spread quickly that there had been an attack on the last picket post on Pennington Road and "four were wounded."

In a very few minutes, Lt. Col. Brethauer was on his horse and moving the Rall regiment up High Street on the double. Brethauer halted his regiment on "the rising ground where the Maidenhead and Pennington roads come together." Col. Rall was in his saddle almost as quickly, after having ordered an aide to send for 20 light dragoons to accompany him. When Rall and the dragoons reached the head of the street, Rall went into conference with Brethauer.

Rall then ordered the 20 dragoons and a part of the Rall regiment to reconnoiter the area beyond where the attack had taken place. They advanced out Pennington Road and also out the road to Johnson's and McKonkey's Ferries but found no enemy, although Brethauer thought he heard unfamiliar noises in the woods. While these troops under Brethauer were out on reconnoiter, Rall visited the guard station on the Trenton-Princeton Road and talked with Ensign Friedrich granted the right to build a road on his own property "from the Ferry on Dellaware known by the name Johnson's Ferry to the Great Road, that Leads from Trenton to Bellmouth . . . about two Chains north of the Eight mile Post from Trenton." (Hunterdon Road Records 1:43) In the road application, it referred to an already existing "lower and upper landing," (ibid) close by. Whether a third landing was built at this time, is not known.

Soon after the road construction work was completed, on May 19, 1767, it is recorded that James Slack "hath rented the Plantation and Ferry belonging to Rutt Johnson." (Hunterdon Tavern Applications 662) Rutt Johnson apparently felt the same financial pinch as did his brother, Robert, for on September 25, 1769, he offered his plantation for sale. In the advertisement, it described the main building on his 240 acre tract as follows: "a large frame house with five rooms on a floor with a cellar underneath, with a large stone kitchen, which is now occupied and has for some years past as a tavern and ferry." (NJA XXVI:507) Rutt seems not to have sold his property at this time, for James Slack's license was renewed as late as May 4, 1777. (Hunterdon Tavern Applications 668)

Samuel McKonkey's Ferry

According to a publication of 1932 titled "Improving Navigation on the Delaware River with some accounts of its Ferries, Bridges, Canals and Floods," the history of McKonkey's Ferry is as follows:

The ferry was established in the late 1600s by Henry Baker who, in 1684, acquired a large tract of land at what is now Washington Crossing, Pennsylvania. The ferry passed to Samuel Baker, a son, and upon the death of Samuel, the ferry was purchased (March 10, 1763) by Samuel Baker Jr.

On December 5, 1774, the ferry was sold to Samuel McKonkey and the name was changed at that time from Baker's Ferry to McKonkey's Ferry. Samuel McKonkey operated the ferry until March 21, 1777, when it was sold to Benjamin Taylor, and it became known as Taylor's Ferry, for whom the town of Taylorsville was named.

APPENDIX C

COLONEL JOHANN GOTTLIEB RALL was 50 at the time of the Battle of Trenton. He was born in 1726, the son of Joachim Georg Rall and Catharina Elisabeth Dreyeich. Johann Rall was so-called "born in the regiment" von Loewenstein, where his father was aide-de-camp. The father progressed in the regiment to lieutenant in 1729, regimental quartermaster in 1733, and captain in 1739. He left the service in 1749 and died in 1771 at Rinteln, Hesse.

Johann, the eldest of at least seven boys, entered his father's regiment March 1, 1740, became ensign in 1741, lieutenant in 1745, captain in 1753, and major in 1760.

In 1762, Rall was transferred to the newly-formed regiment Heldring, with the rank of lieutenant colonel. Rall received his colonelcy April 19, 1771, and was transferred to the grenadier regiment Mansbach, of which regiment he became commander when von Mansbach retired November 6, 1771. The regiment at that time took the name of Rall, for its new commander.

Upon coming to America, the Rall regiment became part of Major General Werner von Mirbach's brigade. Gen. von Mirbach suffered a paralytic stroke after the Battle of Long Island,

and Rall commanded the brigade at the subsequent capture of Ft. Washington, where he performed brilliantly.

As a result of his ability shown at Ft. Washington, Rall, although junior in rank to several other Hessian colonels, was given the official command of the brigade and sent across the North River on November 28, 1776.

COLONEL CARL EMIL ULRICH VON DONOP was 43 at the time of the Battle of Trenton. He was born at castle Woebbel in Lippe, Germany, January 1, 1732, to Friedrich Ulrich von Donop-Steveringen and Antoinette Ernestine von Donop-Woebbel. The father had been a lieutenant colonel in the Danish army. Carl Emil, the younger son in a family of three girls and two boys, began his military career in the Hesse-Cassel grenadiers. By 1760, age 28, he had become a major in the Guards, and in 1766 a colonel of the 1st battalion of Guards, and aide-de-camp and chamberlain of the Landgraf of Hesse-Cassel.

When the Landgraf of Hesse-Cassel (Frederick II.) agreed to assist his cousin George III. of Britain by providing troops at hire to fight the war of independence in the American colonies, von Donop organized the Jaeger corps and three grenadier battalions which he commanded in America.

Note: Biographies of the main contestants on the American side may be found in various published works (such as the Dictionary of American Biography) and therefore, are not included here.

APPENDIX D

Hessian Casualties

	Killed or Missing		Wounded		Captured	
Officers	5	(1)	5	(2)	23	(3)
Non-Coms.	1	(4)	3	(4)	84	(4)
Privates and drums	16	(4)	75	(4)	784	(4)
	22		83		891	(5)

(1) 1 colonel, 1 major, 2 captains, 1 lieutenant
(2) Estimate
(3) Gen. Washington's figures (WW 6:443)
(4) Hessian war trial figures (Lidg. 1148)
(5) Gen. Washington's figure 918, which may have included some of the number the Hessians counted as wounded. (WW 6:444,445 note)

Hessian

Total Trenton Force

Killed or captured (22 plus 891 above)	913	
Escapees to Bordentown (approximately)	600	(6)
Escapees to Princeton	53	(7)
	1566	
British dragoons	20	(8)
	1586	

(6) Von Jungkenn Papers (Cl.L.von J. #1)
(7) Letter Leslie to von Donop (NYPL Ban. 36 Lit AA)
(8) NYPL Ban. 36 Lit. A

Hessian

Rank and File Statistics

by Regiment (9)

	non-coms.	drums	privates
Killed or Mising			
von Lossberg	1		3
von Knyphausen			1
Rall			12
Wounded			
von Lossberg	1		54
von Knyphausen	2		11
Rall			10
Prisoners			
von Lossberg	32	8	238
von Knyphausen	27	7	276
Rall	25		255

(9) Lidg.1148

APPPENDIX E

Washington's General Orders

"Each brigade to be furnished with two good guides. General Stephen's brigade to form the advance party, and to have with them a detachment of the artillery without cannon, provided with spikes and hammers to spike up the enemies' cannon in case of necessity, or to bring them off if it can be effected, the party to be provided with drag-ropes for the purpose of dragging off the cannon. General Stephen is to attack and force the enemy's guards and seize such posts as may prevent them from forming in the streets, and in case they are annoyed from the houses to set them on fire. The brigades of Mercer and Lord Stirling, under the command of Major-General Greene, to support General Stephen. This is the 2d division or left wing of the army and to march by the way of the Pennington road.

"St. Clair's, Glover's and Sargent's brigades, under Major-General Sullivan, to march by the River Road. This is the first division of the army, and to form the right wing. Lord Stirling's brigade to form the reserve of the left wing, and General St. Clair's brigade the reserve of the right wing. These reserves to form a second line in conjunction, or a second line to each division, as circumstances may require. Each brigadier to make the colonels acquainted with the posts of their respective regiments in the brigade, and the major-generals will inform them of the posts of the brigades in the line. Four pieces of artillery to march at the head of each column; three pieces at the head of the second brigade of each division; and two pieces with each of the reserves. The troops to be assembled one mile back of McKonkey's Ferry, and as soon as it begins to grow dark. the troops to be marched to McKonkey's Ferry, and embark on board the boats in following order under the direction of Colonel Knox.

"General Stephen's brigade, with the detachment of artillerymen, to embark first; General Mercer's next; Lord Stirling's next; General Fermoy's next, who will march into the rear of the second division and file off from the Pennington road in such direction that he can with the greatest ease and safety secure the passes between Princeton and Trenton. The guides will be the best judges of this. He is to take two pieces of artillery with him. St. Clair's, Glover's, and Sargent's brigades to embark in order. Immediately upon their debarkation, the whole to form and march in subdivisions from the right. The commanding officers of regiments to observe that the divisions be equal and that proper officers be appointed to each. A profound silence to be enjoined, and no man to quit his ranks on the pain of death. Each brigadier to appoint flanking parties; the reserve brigades to appoint the rear-guards of the columns; the heads of the columns to be appointed to arrive at Trenton at five o'clock.

"Captain Washington and Captain Flahaven, with a party of forty men each, to march before the divisions and post themselves on the road about three miles from Trenton, and make prisoners of all going in or coming out of town.

"General Stephen will appoint a guard to form a chain of sentries round the landing-place at a sufficient distance from the river. to permit the troops to form, this guard not to suffer any person to go in or come out, but to detain all persons who attempt either. This guard to join their brigade when the troops are all over."

Mercer's Brigade Orders

GENERAL MERCER TO COLONEL DURKEE

SIR: 25 Dcr. 1776.

You are to see that your men have three days provisions ready cooked before 12 o'clock this forenoon—the whole fit for duty except a Serjeant and six men to be left with the baggage, and to parade precisely at four in the afternoon with their arms, accoutrements & ammunition in the best order, with their provisions and blankets—you will have them told off in divisions in which order they are to march—eight men a breast, with the officers fixed to their divisions from which they are on no account to separate—no man is to quit his division on pain of instant punishment—each officer is to provide himself with a piece of white paper stuck in his hat for a field mark. You will order your men to assemble and parade them in the valley immediately over the hill on the back of McConkey's Ferry, to remain their for farther orders—a profound silence is to be observed, both by officers and men, and a strict and ready attention paid to whatever orders may be given—in forming the Brigade Co. Durkee takes the right, Co. Stone left, Co. Bradley on the left of Co. Durkee & Co. Rawlings on the Right of Co. Stone—the Line to from & march from the Right—Co. Hutchinson to form by themselves.

Your obt s'v't

H. MERCER.

BIBLIOGRAPHY

Hessian Manuscripts

Hessisches Staatsarchiv (State Archives) Marburg, Germany:

(St. AM 12, 11, 1b) a) Bestand 12, Verzeichnis 11, no. 1b :
Darstellung der Affaire in Trenton durch den Gen. Lt. v. Heister (Report on the affair at Trenton by Lt. Gen. v. Heister)—1777.

(St. AM 12, 11, 1c) b) Bestand 12, Verzeichnis 11, no. 1c :
dto. von den einzelnen Truppenteilen (Report of the Hessian units)—1777.

(Lidg.) c) Bestand 4h, Verzeichnis 328, no. 128-144:
Hessischer Untersuchungsbericht ueber Trenton (Hessian courtmartail upon Trenton) Philadelphia, 1778, April-May New York, 1778, August-October; 1781, Dec. Cassel, Germany, 1782, April.
—Translated transcript in the William van Vleek Lidgerwood Collection, Morristown, N.J., National Historical Park Library, Morristown, N.J. Translated by G. Weintraut, Asst. Writer of Chancellery at Royal State Archives, Marburg, Germany, Ca. 1880.

d) Journals of the Hessian Regiments at Trenton and Bordentown. (1776-1783/4)

(St. AM 12, 11, 2) Bestand 12, Verzeichnis 11, I Ba. no. 2:
Journal des Hochloeblicnen Regiments von Alt-Lossberg

(St. AM 12, 11, 6) Bestand 12, Verzeichnis 11, I Ba. no. 6:
Journal des Infanterie-Regiments von Knyphausen

(St. AM 12, 11, 14) Bestand 12, Verzeichnis 11, I Ba. no. 14:
Journal des Grenadier Bataillons Block, nachher Lengercke

(St. AM 12, 11, 15) Bestand 12, Verzeichnis 11, I Ba. no. 15:
Journal von dem Hochloebl.-Hessischen Grenadier Bataillon olim von Minnigerode, modo von Loewenstein.—Translated by Dr. Ernst Kipping, University of Bonn, Germany. (1964/65)

(Sch. Hol. L) *Ewald*, Johann (von), Tagebuch von dem amerikanischen Kriege (Diary of the American War), 4 vols., mss. One Copy in the library of His Highness Friedrich Ferdinand, Prince of Schleswig-Holstein, Germany, the other known one in private possession in America. Fragment translated by Dr. Ernst Kipping (1964/65)

(RUL Sp.C) *Reuber*, Johannes, Diary of The Revolutionary War, mss. Copy at Rutgers University Library, Special Collections, New Brunswick, N. J. Fragment translated by Dr. Ernst Kipping (1964/65).

(Am. Ger. IV:1:25-33) *Wiederholt*, Andreas, Tagebuch des Capitains . . . , (Diary of captain Wiederholt of the von Knyphausen Regiment), M.D. Learned and C. Grosse ed., in: Americana Germanica, vol. IV, 1, New York, London and Berlin, 1902, p. 25-33 (1776, Dec. 4-28).
—Translated by Dr. Ernst Kipping (1964/65).

(NYPL Ban. 36) Bericht ueber den UeberFall in Trenton (Report on the Raid at Trenton-von Donop Diary. 1776, Dec. 13-31). New York Public Library, Mss. Div., Bancroft Collection, Hessian Manuscripts no. 36.—Translated by Dr. Ernst Kipping (1964/65).

(NYPL Ban. 36) Correspondence between Colonel von Donop and Generals Leslie, Grant, Colonel Rall, and others. (1776, Dec. 13-29). New York Public Library, Mss. Div., Bancroft Collection, Hessian Manuscripts no. 36.—Translated by Dr. Ernst Kipping (1964/65).

(Cl. L Von Jungkenn) Von Jungkenn Manuscripts, Letters and Diaries written to the Hessian State Minister Lt. Gen. Freiherr von Jungkenn by Hessian officers and generals from America. mss. 7 vols. William L. Clements Library, Ann Arbor, Mich.
Fragments translated by Dr. Ernst Kipping (1964/65), and Mr. Hans Mayer, Librarian, Morristown Natl. Hist. Park. (1965).

Miscellaneous

(AA) American Archives, Peter Force, ed., Washington 1837-1853.

(CO) Colonial Office Records, Public Records Office, London.

(BRA) Father Abraham's Pocket Almanac 1775, 1776, 1778 printed by John Dunlap, Phila. (entries by Benjamin Randolph) mss. collection. Philadelphia Historical Society, Philadelphia.

(TRD)	Diary of Captain Thomas Rodney, Historical Society of Delaware, Paper #8 (1888).
(Brun)	Guide of Manuscript Maps in the William L. Clements Library, Christian Brun, ed., Ann Arbor, 1959.
(Dewey)	Dewey, Private John, Military Journal of April 1776–February 1777 (See Matthews American Diaries)
(Glyn)	Glyn, Ensign Thomas, Diary of April 14, 1776–August 17, 1777. Princeton University, Special Collections.
(HRR)	Hunterdon County, N. J. Road Records Book I. Flemington, N. J.
(KP)	The Kemble Papers, New York Historical Society, Collections XVI, XVII, (2 vol.) 1884-85.
(LP)	The Lee Papers, New York Historical Society, Collections IV, V, VI, VII, (4 vol.) 1871-74.
(NJA)	New Jersey Archives, New Jersey Historical Society, Newark, N. J.
(PM)	Pennsylvania Magazine of History and Biography, Historical Society of Pennsylvania, Philadelphia.
(PNJHS)	Proceedings of the New Jersey Historical Society, Newark, New Jersey.
(RA)	Revolution in America, Bernhard A. Uhlendorf, ed. Confidential Letters and Journals 1776-1784 of Adj. Gen. Maj. Baurmeister, New Brunswick, N. J. 1957.
(WW)	The Writings of Washington John C. Fitzpatrick, ed., vol. 6, Sept., 1776–Jan., 1777. Washington, D. C., 1932.

REFERENCES

Chapter I

"The Enemy are . . . "	(WW 6:320)
"It being impossible . . . "	(WW 6:322)
"4000 men . . . "	(WW 6:320)
"about 2000 men . . . "	(WW 6:421)
"I must entreat . . . "	(WW 6:318)
"1200 men . . . "	(WW 6:331)
"went away June . . . "	(BRA 1776)
"When the Enemy . . . "	(WW 6:323)
"about 4000 men . . . "	(KP 1:101)
"good winter quarters . . . "	(Lidg. 2 von Heister)
"advance the army . . . "	(ibid)
"not to advance . . . "	(CO 5:94:31-36)
"General Howe became . . . "	(AA 5:3:1325-1328)
"General Howe went . . . "	(KP 1:102)
"the advantage that . . . "	(CO 5:94:31-36)
"General Howe marched . . . "	(KP 1:102)
"reached the Delaware . . . "	(CO 5:94:31-36)

Chapter II

"Next morning at . . . "	(CO 5:94:31-36)
"if they cross . . . "	(WW 6:339)
"bring our cannon . . . "	(ibid)
"Quarter Brigades in . . . "	(WW 6:343)
"near where his . . . "	(WW 6:365 note)
"Berkleys Summer seat . . . "	(WW 6:335)
"seem to indicate . . . "	(WW 6:342)
"Having sent down . . . "	(WW 6:345)
"I tremble for . . . "	(WW 6:346)
"That, until Congress . . . "	(WW 6:354 note)
"full of the . . . "	(TRD 13)
"marching to Burlington . . . "	(WW 6:355)
"the Enemy are . . . "	(WW 6:402)
"Small straggling Parties . . . "	(KP 1:429)
"It would not . . . "	(NYPL Ban. 36 von Donop Diary)
'improper ambition . . . "	(ibid)
"the usual form . . . "	(NYPL Ban. 36 Lit. B)
"the high ground . . . "	(Lidg. 123 Pauli)

Chapter III

"I can not . . . "	(LP 2:338)
"in one White's . . . "	(KP 1:103)
"undiscovered by the . . . "	(CO 5:94:31-36)
"He himself requested . . . "	(KP 1:103)
"I have so . . . "	(WW 6:370)
"The Campaign having . . . "	(KP 1:425)
"near the main . . . "	(WW 6:364)
"to attempt a . . . "	(WW 6:366)
"Fourteen or Fifteen . . . "	(WW 6:432)
"Let me entreat . . . "	(WW 6:369)
"the enemy were . . . "	(2 NJA 1:243)
"two killed and . . . "	(ibid)
"let those longing . . . "	(NYPL Ban. 36 von Donop Diary)

Chapter IV

"50 Jaegers and . . . "	(NYPL Ban. 36 Lit. A)
"deadly wounded . . . "	(NYPL Ban. 36 von Donop Diary)
"strong cannonade and . . . "	(ibid)
"18 cannon shot . . . "	(ibid)
"four miles above . . . "	(ibid)
"rebel unit of . . . "	(ibid)
"of 220 men . . . "	(St. AM 12, 11, 1c)
"captured three men . . . "	(NYPL Ban. 36 von Donop Diary)
"Colonel Chambers of . . . "	(NYPL Ban. 36 Lit. Y)
"up the Delaware . . . "	(NYPL Ban. 36 von Donop Diary)
"met a rebel . . . "	(ibid)
"Captain Anderson, with . . . "	(AA 5:3:1343, 1344)
"were not held . . . "	(Lidg. 573 von Hanstein)
"necessary for Pennington . . . "	(Lidg. 1128 Matthaeus)
"What if the . . . "	(ibid)
"4000 of the . . . "	(NYPL Ban. 36 Lit. R)
"it is impossible . . . "	(NYPL Ban. 36 Lit. N)
"I am ready . . . "	(ibid)
"three letters . . . "	(NYPL Ban. 36 Lit. R)

"fatigue and alarm . . . "   (ibid)
"had their cartridge . . . "   (St. AM 12, 11, 1c)
"in fact almost . . . "   (NYPL Ban. 36 Lit. R)
"Sentries, Commands, and . . . "(Am. Ger. IV: 1:25-33)

Chapter V

"The duty-time . . . "   (NYPL Ban. 36 von Donop
                                             Diary)
"few or no . . . "   (WW 6:409)
"without Shoes or . . . "   (PM 8:393)
"When I reflect . . . "   (WW 6:411)
"The Cloathing of . . . "   (WW 6:381)
"as soon as . . . "   (WW 6:433)
"Had I entertained . . . "   (ibid)
"but it was . . . "   (St. AM 12, 11, 2)
"between five and . . . "   (WW 6:356)
"about 200 militia . . . "   (AA 5:3:1365)

Chapter VI

"as far as . . . "   (AA 5:3:1360, 1361)
"I hinted to . . . "   (WW 6:428)
"at 9 o'clock . . . "   (TRD 20)
"had determined on . . . "   (ibid)
"he would send . . . "   (ibid)
"Sullivan, Gates, Arnold . . . "(NYPL Ban. 36 Lit. Y)
"fix with Colo. . . . "   (WW 6:429)
"privately communicated   (TRD 21)
   all . . . "
"some of the . . . "   (WW 6:428)
"move forward if . . . "   (WW 6:429)
"the shortness of . . . "   (PM 8:393)
"returned to Bristol . . . "   (ibid)
"The two companies . . . "   (ibid)
"600 men . . . "   (WW 6:447 note)
"the bridge leading . . . "   (WW 6:443)
"about 2400 . . . "   (WW 6:442)
"We are in . . . "   (NYPL Ban. 36 Lit. V)
"at past 11 . . . "   (NYPL Ban. 36 Lit. Y)
"sunday last . . . "   (ibid)
"weak at Trenton . . . "   (ibid)
"I do not . . . "   (ibid)
"send away the . . . "   (Lidg. 1188 Colonels' opinion)

Chapter VII

"50 paces . . . "   (Lidg. 995 Engelhard)
"duty was mixed . . . "   (Lidg. 352 Grebe)
"At 8 o'clock . . . "   (St. AM 12, 11, 6)
"four were wounded . . . "   (Lidg. 702 Wiederholt)
"the rising ground . . . "   (Lidg. 997 Engelhard)
"with nine men . . . "   (Am. Ger. IV:1:25-33)
"in front of . . . "   (Lidg. 702 Wiederholt)
"would not have . . . "   (TRD 20)
"in the Wrights . . . "   (Glyn 35)
"one mile back . . . "   (Appendix E)
"lower and upper . . . "   (HRR 1:43)
"as soon as . . . "   (WW 6:442)
"create as great . . . "   (WW 6:441)
"continuous rain and . . . "   (St. AM 12, 11, 15)
"east northeast . . . "   (PM 8:258, 259)
"About dark . . . "   (TRD 22)

"Neshaminy Ferry . . . "   (ibid)
"advance party of . . . "   (ibid)
"the light infantry . . . "   (PM 8:393)
"Grand Parade at . . . "   (PM 8:758, 759)
"about 1800 men . . . "   (WW 6:451)
"they set out . . . "   (PM 8:258, 259)
"rather round about . . . "   (PM 38:276)
"Light infantry battalion . . . "(TRD 22)
"when the 1st . . . "   (PM 38:276)
"about 600 light . . . "   (TRD 23)
"everything in his . . . "   (WW 6:443)

Chapter VIII

"by 12 o'clock . . . "   (WW 6:442)
"near four, before . . . "   (ibid)
"the east northeast . . . "   (PM 8:258, 259)
"very cold . . . "   (ibid)
"slippery . . . "   (2 NJA 1:247)
"file off from . . . "   (Appendix E)
"there came a . . . "   (PM 8:394)
"under woolen blankets . . . "   (St. AM 12, 11, 6)
"The Enemy's advance . . . "   (WW 6:442)
"About an hour . . . "   (Am. Ger. IV:1:25-33)
"a heavy fire . . . "   (Lidg. 714 Wiederholt)
"the infantry picket . . . "   (Lidg. 312 Bauer)
"the rebels were . . . "   (Lidg. 314 Bauer)
"toward the town . . . "   (ibid)

Chapter IX

"On the first . . . "   (Lidg. 261 Counsellor)
"one after the . . . "   (ibid)
"still in the . . . "   (Lidg. 1135 Matthaeus)
"a large open . . . "   (Lidg. 504 Schwabe)
"before their respective . . . "   (Lidg. 503 Schwabe)
"when Col. Rall . . . "   (Lidg. 1007 Engelhard)
"no escort whatever . . . "   (Lidg. 1012 Engelhard)
"from the place . . . "   (Lidg. 1008 Engelhard)
"from behind Rall's . . . "   (Lidg. 1010 Engelhard)
"out of town . . . "   (St. AM 12, 11, 6)
"Colo. Hands and . . . "   (WW 6:443 note)
"should march about . . . "   (Lidg. 246 Piel)
"Yes . . . "   (ibid)
"to come with . . . "   (Lidg. 564 Volprecht)
"alle was meine . . . "   (RUL Sp. C)
"cartridges of the . . . "   (St. AM 12, 11, 1c)
"their touch-pans . . . "   (ibid)
"ordered Lord Stirling . . . "   (WW 6:443 note)
"advanced on the . . . "   (Lidg. 506, 507 Schwabe)
"deadly wounded twice . . . "   (St. AM 12, 11, 6)
"to make a . . . "   (Lidg. 615 Scheffer)
"like a half-moon . . . "   (St. AM 12, 11, 1c)
"mixed together . . . "   (Lidg. 615 Scheffer)
"burst into the . . . "   (Lidg. 622 Scheffer)
"at a distance . . . "   (Lidg. 583 von Hanstein)
"in German and . . . "   (Lidg. 681 Fischer)
"came galloping up . . . "   (Lidg. 583 von Hanstein)
"an adjutant general . . . "   (Lidg. 1145 Matthaeus)
"back into town . . . "   (Lidg. 555 von Altenbockum)
"in the swamp . . . "   (St. AM 12, 11, 6)
"two enemy battalions . . . "   (ibid)
"My dear sirs . . . "   (Lidg. 565 Volprecht)

"a white handkerchief . . . "   (Lidg. 710 Wiederholt)
"up to their . . . "   (Lidg. 770 Baum)
"steep bank . . . "   (St. AM 12, 11, 6)

"a brigade of . . . "   (Lidg. 744 Sobbe)
"two columns with . . . "   (ibid)
"ford to cross . . . "   (St. AM 12, 11, 6)
"ordered through the . . . "   (Dewey 280)
"Gen. Stirling wished . . . "   (Lidg. 905 von Biesenrodt)
"capitulate to Gen. . . . "   (Lidg. 265 Counsellor)
"Lasted about two . . . "   (Lidg. 584 von Hanstein)

Chapter X

"Fifty men and . . . "   (NYPL Ban. 36 Lit. AA)
"suffered incredible fatigue . . ."(Lidg. 772 Baum)
"over 600 . . . "   (Cl. L von Jungkenn 1)
"a good hour . . . "   (Lidg. 317 Bauer)
"not one single . . . "   (Lidg. 698 Mueller)
"lot of little . . . "   (Lidg. 658 Zimmerman)
"I received the . . . "   (Cl. L von Jungkenn 1)
"stationed just across . . . "   (ibid)
"many more fugitives . . . "   (ibid)
"as quickly as . . . "   (RUL Sp. C)
"but found no . . . "   (WW 6:444)
"where they were . . . "   (St. AM 12, 11, 2)
"in the ferry-house . . . "   (Am. Ger. IV:1:25-33)
"very carefully . . . "   (St. AM 12, 11, 2)
"not more than . . . "   (WW 6:446)
"our loss is . . . "   (WW 6:443)
"carried into the . . . "   (Lidg. 509 Schwabe)
"918 prisoners, 6 . . . "   (WW 6:444, 445 note)

★   ★   ★